FIREFLIES

RABINDRANATH TAGORE

Decorations by
BORIS ARTZYBASHEFF

COLLIER BOOKS
Macmillan Publishing Company
New York

Macmillan Publishing Company
866 Third Avenue, New York, N.Y. 10022
Collier Macmillan Canada, Inc.

Library of Congress Cataloging in Publication Data
Tagore, Rabindranath, Sir, 1861-1941.
Fireflies.
Reprint of the ed. published by Macmillan, New York.
I. Title.
PR9499.3.T34F5 1975   891'.44'14   75-15656
ISBN 0-02-089640-9

9
Printed in the United States of America

FIREFLIES had their origin in China and Japan where thoughts were very often claimed from me in my handwriting on fans and pieces of silk.

My fancies are fireflies,—
Specks of living light
   twinkling in the dark.

The voice of wayside pansies,
    that do not attract the careless glance,
      murmurs in these desultory lines.

In the drowsy dark caves of the mind
  dreams build their nest with fragments
    dropped from day's caravan.

Spring scatters the petals of flowers
  that are not for the fruits of the future,
    but for the moment's whim.

Joy freed from the bond of earth's slumber
   rushes into numberless leaves,
      and dances in the air for a day.

My words that are slight
　　may lightly dance upon time's waves
　　　　when my works heavy with import have
　　　　　　gone down.

Mind's underground moths
grow filmy wings
and take a farewell flight
in the sunset sky.

The butterfly counts not months but moments,
and has time enough.

My thoughts, like sparks, ride on winged
    surprises,
    carrying a single laughter.
The tree gazes in love at its own beautiful
    shadow
    which yet it never can grasp.

Let my love, like sunlight, surround you
 and yet give you illumined freedom.

Days are coloured bubbles
	that float upon the surface of fathomless
		night.

My offerings are too timid to claim your
    remembrance,
    and therefore you may remember them.

Leave out my name from the gift
if it be a burden,
but keep my song.

[18]

April, like a child,
    writes hieroglyphs on dust with flowers,
        wipes them away and forgets.

Memory, the priestess,
   kills the present
and offers its heart to the shrine of the dead
      past.

From the solemn gloom of the temple
children run out to sit in the dust,
God watches them play
and forgets the priest.

My mind starts up at some flash
    on the flow of its thoughts
  like a brook at a sudden liquid note of its
      own
    that is never repeated.

In the mountain, stillness surges up
to explore its own height;
in the lake, movement stands still
to contemplate its own depth.

The departing night's one kiss
on the closed eyes of morning
glows in the star of dawn.

Maiden, thy beauty is like a fruit
  which is yet to mature,
    tense with an unyielding secret.

Sorrow that has lost its memory
  is like the dumb dark hours
    that have no bird songs
      but only the cricket's chirp.

Bigotry tries to keep truth safe in its hand
    with a grip that kills it.
Wishing to hearten a timid lamp
    great night lights all her stars.

Though he holds in his arms the earth-bride,
the sky is ever immensely away.

God seeks comrades and claims love,
    the Devil seeks slaves and claims obedi-
        ence.

The soil in return for her service
  keeps the tree tied to her,
    the sky asks nothing and leaves it free.

Jewel-like the immortal
   does not boast of its length of years
      but of the scintillating point of its
         moment.

The child ever dwells in the mystery
        of ageless time,
unobscured by the dust of history.

A light laughter in the steps of creation
carries it swiftly across time.

One who was distant came near to me in the
    morning,
  and still nearer when taken away by night.

White and pink oleanders meet
   and make merry in different dialects.

When peace is active sweeping its dirt,
    it is storm.

The lake lies low by the hill,
　　a tearful entreaty of love
　　　　at the foot of the inflexible.

There smiles the Divine Child
　　among his playthings of unmeaning clouds
　　and ephemeral lights and shadows.

The breeze whispers to the lotus,
   "What is thy secret?"
      "It is myself," says the lotus,
         "Steal it and I disappear!"

The freedom of the storm and the bondage
     of the stem
  join hands in the dance of swaying
     branches.

The jasmine's lisping of love to the sun
is her flowers.

The tyrant claims freedom to kill freedom
and yet to keep it for himself.

Gods, tired of their paradise, envy man.

Clouds are hills in vapour,
   hills are clouds in stone,—
      a phantasy in time's dream.

While God waits for His temple to be built
  of love,
    men bring stones.

I touch God in my song
    as the hill touches the far-away sea
      with its waterfall.

Light finds her treasure of colours
    through the antagonism of clouds.

My heart to-day smiles at its past night of tears
like a wet tree glistening in the sun
after the rain is over.

I have thanked the trees that have made my
      life fruitful,
  but have failed to remember the grass
    that has ever kept it green.

The one without second is emptiness,
the other one makes it true.

Life's errors cry for the merciful beauty
    that can modulate their isolation
        into a harmony with the whole.

They expect thanks for the banished nest
because their cage is shapely and secure.

In love I pay my endless debt to thee
for what thou art.

The pond sends up its lyrics from its dark
    in lilies,
    and the sun says, they are good.

Your calumny against the great is impious,
    it hurts yourself;
  against the small it is mean,
      for it hurts the victim.

The first flower that blossomed on this earth
was an invitation to the unborn song.

Dawn—the many-coloured flower—fades,
and then the simple light-fruit,
the sun appears.

The muscle that has a doubt of its wisdom
throttles the voice that would cry.

The wind tries to take the flame by storm
    only to blow it out.

Life's play is swift,
    Life's playthings fall behind one by one
        and are forgotten.

My flower, seek not thy paradise
in a fool's buttonhole.

Thou hast risen late, my crescent moon,
but my night bird is still awake to greet
thee.

Darkness is the veiled bride
    silently waiting for the errant light
        to return to her bosom.

Trees are the earth's endless effort to speak
to the listening heaven.

The burden of self is lightened
when I laugh at myself.

The weak can be terrible
  because they try furiously to appear strong.

The wind of heaven blows,
  The anchor desperately clutches the mud,
    and my boat is beating its breast against
      the chain.

The spirit of death is one,
    the spirit of life is many.
When God is dead religion becomes one.

The blue of the sky longs for the earth's green,
    the wind between them sighs, "Alas."
Day's pain muffled by its own glare,
    burns among stars in the night.

The stars crowd round the virgin night
in silent awe at her loneliness
that can never be touched.

The cloud gives all its gold
to the departing sun
and greets the rising moon
with only a pale smile.

He who does good comes to the temple gate,
he who loves reaches the shrine.

Flower, have pity for the worm,
　　it is not a bee,
　　　　its love is a blunder and a burden.

With the ruins of terror's triumph
  children build their doll's house.

The lamp waits through the long day of
    neglect
  for the flame's kiss in the night.

Feathers in the dust lying lazily content
have forgotten their sky.

The flower which is single
need not envy the thorns
that are numerous.

The world suffers most from the disinterested
        tyranny
  of its well-wisher.

We gain freedom when we have paid the full
      price
  for our right to live.

Your careless gifts of a moment,
    like the meteors of an autumn night,
        catch fire in the depth of my being.

The faith waiting in the heart of a seed
    promises a miracle of life
        which it cannot prove at once.

Spring hesitates at winter's door,
  but the mango blossom rashly runs out to
    him
      before her time and meets her doom.

The world is the ever-changing foam
that floats on the surface of a sea of silence.

The two separated shores mingle their voices
in a song of unfathomed tears.

As a river in the sea,
   work finds its fulfilment
      in the depth of leisure.

I lingered on my way till thy cherry tree lost
    its blossom,
    but the azalea brings to me, my love, thy
    forgiveness.

Thy shy little pomegranate bud,
  blushing to-day behind her veil,
    will burst into a passionate flower
      to-morrow when I am away.

The clumsiness of power spoils the key,
and uses the pickaxe.

Birth is from the mystery of night
   into the greater mystery of day.

These paper boats of mine are meant to dance
    on the ripples of hours,
        and not to reach any destination.

Migratory songs wing from my heart
and seek their nests in your voice of love.

The sea of danger, doubt and denial
around man's little island of certainty
challenges him to dare the unknown.

Love punishes when it forgives,
   and injured beauty by its awful silence.

You live alone and unrecompensed
  because they are afraid of your great worth.

The same sun is newly born in new lands
in a ring of endless dawns.

God's world is ever renewed by death,
  a Titan's ever crushed by its own existence.

The glow-worm while exploring the dust
never knows that stars are in the sky.

The tree is of to-day, the flower is old,
it brings with it the message
of the immemorial seed.

Each rose that comes brings me greetings
    from the Rose of an eternal spring.
God honours me when I work,
    He loves me when I sing.

My love of to-day finds no home
    in the nest deserted by yesterday's love.

The fire of pain traces for my soul
    a luminous path across her sorrow.

The grass survives the hill
through its resurrections from countless
deaths.

Thou hast vanished from my reach
    leaving an impalpable touch in the blue of
        the sky,
        an invisible image in the wind moving
        among the shadows.

In pity for the desolate branch
    spring leaves to it a kiss that fluttered in a
        lonely leaf.

The shy shadow in the garden
  loves the sun in silence,
    Flowers guess the secret, and smile,
      while the leaves whisper.

I leave no trace of wings in the air,
    but I am glad I have had my flight.

The fireflies, twinkling among leaves,
    make the stars wonder.

The mountain remains unmoved
at its seeming defeat by the mist.

While the rose said to the sun,
 "I shall ever remember thee,"
  her petals fell to the dust.

Hills are the earth's gesture of despair
for the unreachable.

Though the thorn in thy flower pricked me,
     O Beauty,
          I am grateful.

The world knows that the few
are more than the many.

Let not my love be a burden on you, my
      friend,
   know that it pays itself.

Dawn plays her lute before the gate of darkness,
and is content to vanish when the sun
comes out.

Beauty is truth's smile
    when she beholds her own face
        in a perfect mirror.

The dew-drop knows the sun
only within its own tiny orb.

Forlorn thoughts from the forsaken hives of
    all ages,
  swarming in the air, hum round my heart
    and seek my voice.

The desert is imprisoned in the wall
of its unbounded barrenness.

In the thrill of little leaves
   I see the air's invisible dance,
     and in their glimmering
       the secret heart-beats of the sky.

You are like a flowering tree,
   amazed when I praise you for your gifts.

The earth's sacrificial fire
   flames up in her trees,
      scattering sparks in flowers.

Forests, the clouds of earth,
   hold up to the sky their silence,
      and clouds from above come down
     in resonant showers.

The world speaks to me in pictures,
my soul answers in music.

The sky tells its beads all night
on the countless stars
in memory of the sun.

The darkness of night, like pain, is dumb,
the darkness of dawn, like peace, is silent.

Pride engraves his frowns in stones,
 love offers her surrender in flowers.

The obsequious brush curtails truth
in deference to the canvas which is narrow.

The hill in its longing for the far-away sky
wishes to be like the cloud
with its endless urge of seeking.

To justify their own spilling of ink
they spell the day as night.

Profit smiles on goodness
    when the good is profitable.

In its swelling pride
   the bubble doubts the truth of the sea,
      and laughs and bursts into emptiness.

Love is an endless mystery,
for it has nothing else to explain it.

My clouds, sorrowing in the dark,
forget that they themselves
have hidden the sun.

Man discovers his own wealth
  when God comes to ask gifts of him.

You leave your memory as a flame
to my lonely lamp of separation.

I came to offer thee a flower,
  but thou must have all my garden,—
    It is thine.

The picture—a memory of light
treasured by the shadow.

It is easy to make faces at the sun,
  He is exposed by his own light in all
    directions.

Love remains a secret even when spoken,
  for only a lover truly knows that he is loved.

History slowly smothers its truth,
but hastily struggles to revive it
in the terrible penance of pain.

My work is rewarded in daily wages,
I wait for my final value in love.

Beauty knows to say, "Enough,"
    barbarism clamours for still more.

God loves to see in me, not his servant,
but himself who serves all.

The darkness of night is in harmony with day,
the morning of mist is discordant.

In the bounteous time of roses love is wine,—
   it is food in the famished hour
      when their petals are shed.

An unknown flower in a strange land
  speaks to the poet:
    "Are we not of the same soil, my lover?"

I am able to love my God
    because He gives me freedom to deny Him.

My untuned strings beg for music
   in their anguished cry of shame.

The worm thinks it strange and foolish
that man does not eat his books.

The clouded sky to-day bears the vision
   of the shadow of a divine sadness
      on the forehead of brooding eternity.

The shade of my tree is for passers-by,
its fruit for the one for whom I wait.

Flushed with the glow of sunset
earth seems like a ripe fruit
ready to be harvested by night.

Light accepts darkness for his spouse
for the sake of creation.

The reed waits for his master's breath,
   the Master goes seeking for his reed.

To the blind pen the hand that writes is
     unreal,
    its writing unmeaning.

The sea smites his own barren breast
  because he has no flowers to offer to the
    moon.

The greed for fruit misses the flower.

God in His temple of stars
    waits for man to bring him his lamp.

The fire restrained in the tree fashions flowers.
Released from bonds, the shameless flame
dies in barren ashes.

The sky sets no snare to capture the moon,
   it is her own freedom which binds her.
The light that fills the sky
   seeks its limit in a dew-drop on the grass.

Wealth is the burden of bigness,
Welfare the fulness of being.

The razor-blade is proud of its keenness
when it sneers at the sun.

The butterfly has leisure to love the lotus,
not the bee busily storing honey.

Child, thou bringest to my heart
  the babble of the wind and the water,
    the flowers' speechless secrets, the clouds'
      dreams,
      the mute gaze of wonder of the morn-
        ing sky.

The rainbow among the clouds may be great but the little butterfly among the bushes is greater.

The mist weaves her net round the morning,
captivates him, and makes him blind.

The Morning Star whispers to Dawn,
  "Tell me that you are only for me."
    "Yes," she answers,
      "And also only for that nameless
      flower."

The sky remains infinitely vacant
    for earth there to build its heaven
        with dreams.

Perhaps the crescent moon smiles in doubt
at being told that it is a fragment
awaiting perfection.

Let the evening forgive the mistakes of the
    day
    and thus win peace for herself.

Beauty smiles in the confinement of the bud,
in the heart of a sweet incompleteness.

Your   flitting love lightly brushed with its
      wings
      my sun-flower
   and never asked if it was ready to surrender
      its honey.

Leaves are silences
    around flowers which are their words.

The tree bears its thousand years
   as one large majestic moment.

My offerings are not for the temple at the end
of the road,
but for the wayside shrines
that surprise me at every bend.

Your smile, my love, like the smell of a
        strange flower,
    is simple and inexplicable.

Death laughs when the merit of the dead is
    exaggerated
  for it swells his store with more than he can
    claim.

The sigh of the shore follows in vain
the breeze that hastens the ship
across the sea.

Truth loves its limits,
for there it meets the beautiful.

Between the shores of Me and Thee
    there is the loud ocean, my own surging
       self,
        which I long to cross.

The right to possess boasts foolishly
of its right to enjoy.

The rose is a great deal more
than a blushing apology for the thorn.

Day offers to the silence of stars
his golden lute to be tuned
for the endless life.

The wise know how to teach,
the fool how to smite.

The centre is still and silent in the heart
of an eternal dance of circles.

The judge thinks that he is just when he
    compares
  the oil of another's lamp
    with the light of his own.

The captive flower in the King's wreath
smiles bitterly when the meadow-flower
envies her.

Its store of snow is the hill's own burden,
    its outpouring of streams is borne by all the
        world.

Listen to the prayer of the forest
for its freedom in flowers.

Let your love see me
　　even through the barrier of nearness.

The spirit of work in creation is there
to carry and help the spirit of play.

To carry the burden of the instrument,
    count the cost of its material,
        and never to know that it is for music,
            is the tragedy of deaf life.

Faith is the bird that feels the light
  and sings when the dawn is still dark.

I bring to thee, night, my day's empty cup,
to be cleansed with thy cool darkness
for a new morning's festival.

The mountain fir, in its rustling,
   modulates the memory of its fights with the
      storm
         into a hymn of peace.

God honoured me with his fight
   when I was rebellious,
      He ignored me when I was languid.

The sectarian thinks
  that he has the sea
    ladled into his private pond.

In the shady depth of life
    are the lonely nests of memories
      that shrink from words.

Let my love find its strength
in the service of day,
its peace in the union of night.

Life sends up in blades of grass
its silent hymn of praise
to the unnamed Light.

The stars of night are to me
  the memorials of my day's faded flowers.

Open thy door to that which must go,
for the loss becomes unseemly when
obstructed.

True end is not in the reaching of the limit,
but in a completion which is limitless.

The shore whispers to the sea:

> "Write to me what thy waves struggle to
> say."

The sea writes in foam again and again
> and wipes off the lines in a boisterous
> despair.

Let the touch of thy finger thrill my life's
    strings
  and make the music thine and mine.

The inner world rounded in my life like a
    fruit,
  matured in joy and sorrow,
    will drop into the darkness of the orig-
      inal soil
      for some further course of creation.

Form is in Matter, rhythm in Force,
meaning in the Person.

There are seekers of wisdom and seekers of
      wealth,
  I seek thy company so that I may sing.

As the tree its leaves, I shed my words on the
earth.

let my thoughts unuttered flower in thy
silence.

My faith in truth, my vision of the perfect,
help thee, Master, in thy creation.

All the delights that I have felt
 in life's fruits and flowers
  let me offer to thee at the end of the feast,
   in a perfect union of love.

Some have thought deeply and explored the
meaning of thy truth,
and they are great;
I have listened to catch the music of thy
play,
and I am glad.

The tree is a winged spirit
　　released from the bondage of seed,
　　　pursuing its adventure of life
　　　across the unknown.

The lotus offers its beauty to the heaven,
the grass its service to the earth.

The sun's kiss mellows into abandonment
    the miserliness of the green fruit clinging
       to its stem.

The flame met the earthen lamp in me,
and what a great marvel of light!

Mistakes live in the neighbourhood of truth
and therefore delude us.

The cloud laughed at the rainbow
  saying that it was an upstart
    gaudy in its emptiness.
The rainbow calmly answered,
  "I am as inevitably real as the sun himself."

Let me not grope in vain in the dark
but keep my mind still in the faith
that the day will break
and truth will appear
in its simplicity.

Through the silent night
    I hear the returning vagrant hopes of the
        morning
        knock at my heart.

My new love comes
   bringing to me the eternal wealth of the
      old.

The earth gazes at the moon and wonders
that she should have all her music in her
smile.

Day with its glare of curiosity
puts the stars to flight.

My mind has its true union with thee, O sky,
   at the window which is mine own,
      and not in the open
         where thou hast thy sole kingdom.

Man claims God's flowers as his own
  when he weaves them in a garland.

The buried city, laid bare to the sun of a new
age,
is ashamed that it has lost all its songs.

Like my heart's pain that has long missed its
      meaning,
the sun's rays robed in dark
hide themselves under the ground.
    Like my heart's pain at love's sudden touch,
    they change their veil at the spring's call
    and come out in the carnival of colours,
        in flowers and leaves.

My life's empty flute
   waits for its final music
      like the primal darkness
         before the stars came out.

Emancipation from the bondage of the soil
is no freedom for the tree.

The tapestry of life's story is woven
with the threads of life's ties
ever joining and breaking.

Those thoughts of mine that are never cap-
tured by words
perch upon my songs and dance.

My soul to-night loses itself
   in the silent heart of a tree
      standing alone among the whispers of
        immensity.

Pearl shells cast up by the sea
    on death's barren beach,—
  a magnificent wastefulness of creative life.

The sunlight opens for me the world's gate,
 love's light its treasure.

My life like the reed with its stops,
    has its play of colours
        through the gaps in its hopes and gains.

Let not my thanks to thee
rob my silence of its fuller homage.

Life's aspirations come
in the guise of children.

The faded flower sighs
    that spring has vanished for ever.

In my life's garden
    my wealth has been of the shadows and
        lights
    that are never gathered and stored.

The fruit that I have gained for ever
    is that which thou hast accepted.

The jasmine knows the sun to be her brother
in the heaven.

Light is young, the ancient light;
    shadows are of the moment, they are born
        old.

I feel that the ferry of my songs at the day's
      end
   will bring me across to the other shore
     from where I shall see.

The butterfly flitting from flower to flower
  ever remains mine,
    I lose the one that is netted by me.

Your voice, free bird, reaches my sleeping
       nest,
  and my drowsy wings dream
    of a voyage to the light
      above the clouds.

I miss the meaning of my own part
   in the play of life
because I know not the parts
    that others play.

The flower sheds all its petals
and finds the fruit.

I leave my songs behind me
  to the bloom of the ever-returning honey-
     suckles
    and the joy of the wind from the south.

Dead leaves when they lose themselves in soil
take part in the life of the forest.

The mind ever seeks its words
   from its sounds and silence
      as the sky from its darkness and light.

The unseen dark plays on his flute
and the rhythm of light
eddies into stars and suns,
into thoughts and dreams.

My songs are to sing
  that I have loved Thy singing.

When the voice of the Silent touches my
   words
I know him and therefore I know myself.

My last salutations are to them
who knew me imperfect and loved me.

Love's gift cannot be given,
it waits to be accepted.

When death comes and whispers to me,
"Thy days are ended,"
let me say to him, "I have lived in love
and not in mere time."
He will ask, "Will thy songs remain?"
I shall say, "I know not, but this I know
that often when I sang I found my eternity."

"Let me light my lamp,"
   says the star,
      "And never debate
if it will help to remove the darkness."

Before the end of my journey
     may I reach within myself
          the one which is the all,
               leaving the outer shell
     to float away with the drifting multitude
          upon the current of chance and change.